Immigration

Identifying Propaganda Techniques

Immigration

Identifying Propaganda Techniques

Curriculum Consultant: JoAnne Buggey, Ph.D.
College of Education, University of Minnesota

By Bonnie Szumski

OPPOSING JUNIORS VIEWPOINTS

Greenhaven Press, Inc.
Post Office Box 289009
San Diego, CA 92198-0009

Titles in the opposing viewpoints juniors series:

Smoking   Death Penalty
Gun Control   Drugs and Sports
Animal Rights   Toxic Wastes
AIDS   Patriotism
Alcohol   Working Mothers
Immigration   Terrorism

Cover photo: Chuck Fishman/TIME Magazine

Library of Congress Cataloging-in-Publication Data

Szumski, Bonnie, 1958–
    Immigration : identifying propaganda techniques / by Bonnie
Szumski.
       p.   cm. — (Opposing viewpoints juniors)
    Summary: Presents opposing viewpoints on three immigration issues:
should illegal immigration be stopped; should legal immigration be
restricted, and does bilingual education benefit non-English
speaking children. The reader may practice distinguishing between
objective fact telling and propaganda techniques.
    ISBN 0-89908-639-X
    1. United States—Emigration and immigration—Government policy—
Juvenile literature.   [1. United States—Emigration and
immigration—Government policy. 2. Critical thinking.]   I. Title.
II. Series.
JV6493.S98 1989
325.73—dc20   89-7508
                                                     CIP
                                                        AC

CONTENTS

An Introduction to
Opposing Viewpoints

When people disagree, it is hard to figure out who is right. You may decide one person is right just because the person is your friend or a relative. But this is not a very good reason to agree or disagree with someone. It is better if you try to understand why these people disagree. On what main points do the two people disagree? Read or listen to each person's argument carefully. Separate the facts and opinions that each person presents. Finally, decide which argument best matches what you think. This process, examining an argument without emotion, is part of what critical thinking is all about.

This is not easy. Many things make it hard to understand and form opinions. People's values, ages, and experiences all influence the way they think. This is why learning to read and think critically is an invaluable skill. Opposing Viewpoints Juniors books will help

you learn and practice skills to improve your ability to read critically. By reading opposing views on an issue, you will become familiar with methods people use to attempt to convince you that their point of view is right. And you will learn to separate the authors' opinions from the facts they present.

Each Opposing Viewpoints Juniors book focuses on one critical thinking skill that will help you judge the views presented. Some of these skills are telling fact from opinion, recognizing propaganda techniques, and locating and analyzing the main idea. These skills will allow you to examine opposing viewpoints more easily. Each viewpoint in this book is paraphrased from the original to make it easier to read. The viewpoints are placed in a running debate and are always placed with the pro view first.

What Are Propaganda Techniques?

Propaganda is information presented in an attempt to influence people. In this Opposing Viewpoints Juniors book you will be asked to identify and study several common propaganda techniques. Some of these techniques appeal to your ability to think logically while others appeal to your emotions. As an example, a car salesperson who is telling you about a small economy car may say, "This car gets much better gas mileage than any other car in its class." The salesperson's argument is based on his belief that you will make your car-buying decision logically. You will compare practical considerations such as mileage and initial cost. Another example is a car salesperson who is telling you about a snazzy Maserati: "This car is the best-looking, fastest car ever made." Her argument for buying the Maserati is based on her belief that you are considering such a car not for its practical qualities but because it excites you and is a status symbol.

In the examples above, the objective of both salespeople is to encourage you to buy a car. Both try to get you to focus on the most appealing quality of their cars—economy in the first example, flashiness in the second. Both ignore the disadvantages of their cars. In both cases, making a wise buying decision would mean getting more information. Since the car salespeople's objective is to get you to buy *their* car, you would need more objective sources, such as *Consumer Reports* magazine, to find out more facts.

DISTRACTING THE READER

All propaganda techniques, like those used by the car salespeople, distract the listener or reader from the complete picture. People who use propaganda techniques encourage you to look only at the factors that are important to accepting their argument as true.

Authors and speakers often use misleading propaganda techniques instead of offering legitimate proof for their arguments. The propaganda will be offered as a reason to believe the argument, but in reality will be weak, distracting, or irrelevant reasons. This Opposing Viewpoints Juniors book will focus on telling the difference between legitimate reasons to believe a particular argument and propaganda techniques that are used to mislead or distract you.

It is important to learn to recognize these techniques, expecially when reading and evaluating differing opinions. This is because people who feel strongly about an issue use many of these techniques when attempting to persuade others to agree with their opinion. Some of these persuasive techniques may be relevant to your decision to agree or not, but others will not be. It is important to sift through the information, weeding the proof from the false reasoning.

While there are many types of propaganda techniques, this book will focus on three of them. These are *testimonial, card stacking,* and *scare tactics.* Examples of these techniques are given below:

Testimonial—quoting or paraphrasing an authority or celebrity to support one's own argument. Often, the celebrity is not qualified to express an opinion on the subject. For example, movie stars are often used to recommend a product they may know nothing about. An actor may be dressed in a white medical coat to recommend a pain medication in a television commercial. The producers of the commercial believe you will assume the actor in a white medical coat is a doctor. They hope you will buy the pain medication because you trust doctors' opinions. But the truth is that the actor is not a doctor, has no knowledge of medicine, and is in no position to express an informed opinion. The commercial is deceptive—it asks you to accept the advice of someone who is not a true authority on the topic.

Testimonials can be used in a positive way as well. If the person quoted is truly an authority on the subject being talked about, the testimonial can support an argument. Quoting comedian Richard Pryor about how drugs almost ruined his life is an example of a testimonial that presents a legitimate reason to believe drugs can be dangerous. Pryor *is* an authority on this subject and can give advice based on his personal experience.

Card stacking—using half-truths or whole truths that have no point in the discussion. Card-stacking techniques include distorting or twisting facts, giving only the facts that are favorable to your argument, or quoting someone incompletely or out of context.

An example is "four out of five dentists surveyed recommend sugarless gum for their patients who chew gum." At first, this statement seems to say that most dentists believe people should chew sugarless gum. In fact, this statement is an example of card stacking for a number of reasons: For one thing, we do not know how many dentists were surveyed. If only five were surveyed, this statistic is not very meaningful. Also, this statement is actually saying that dentists recommend sugarless gum only if their patients already chew gum. That is not the same as saying everyone should chew sugarless gum.

Scare tactics—the threat that if you do not do or believe this, something terrible will happen. People using this technique write or say alarming words and phrases to persuade you to believe their argument.

An example is "illegal immigration endangers every worker in the United States." The person quoted does not say *how* illegal immigration will endanger everyone. The purpose of the statement is to scare you into believing his argument. The person wants you to make a decision based on fear about the issue, not on logical reasoning.

SOUND REASONING VS. PROPAGANDA

When reading differing arguments, then, there is a lot to think about. Are the authors giving sound reasons for their points of view? Or do they distort the importance of their arguments through card stacking, use testimonials deceptively, or play on your fear and emotions through scare tactics?

We asked two students to give their opinions on the immigration issue. Look for examples of testimonial, card stacking, and scare tactics in their arguments:

I think immigration is good for the U.S.

Immigration helps the U.S. After all, America is a country of immigrants. Practically every family who lives in the U.S. had ancestors who once immigrated here. My last name is Polski, and my grandparents were born in Poland. My grandmother says Poland was a rotten place to live and they would probably have been killed if they had stayed there. She says the U.S. is the freest, most open country in the world.

If the U.S. didn't allow people from other countries to come here, we'd have to take down the Statue of Liberty. We're the best country because we let all kinds of people live here. That's what the U.S. stands for—letting poor, hungry, and unhappy people, like my grandparents, come here.

I think immigration is bad for the U.S.

Immigration might have been O.K. a long time ago, but not now. Everything is so crowded here now. I live in California, and there are lots and lots of immigrants who live here. My dad says that it's getting so crowded that people are having a hard time getting jobs. He also says a lot of these people live off welfare, and he pays for them through his taxes. I don't think that's right. A lot of these immigrants don't even speak English. In school, I can't even understand what they say.

Sure, a long time ago the U.S. needed people to come here. But now there aren't enough jobs or houses to go around. I think the U.S. should allow only a few people to come here now. Otherwise, a lot of people won't be able to find work and will have to live on the streets.

ANALYZING THE
SAMPLE VIEWPOINTS

Brad and Julie have very different opinions about immigration. Both of them use examples of propaganda techniques in their arguments:

Brad:

TESTIMONIAL

His grandmother says immigration should be allowed.

CARD STACKING

The U.S. is the freest, most open country in the world; we're the best country; the U.S. stands for freedom.

Julie:

TESTIMONIAL

Dad says that people have a hard time finding jobs because of immigration.

SCARE TACTICS

If we don't stop immigration, a lot of people will be living on the streets.

In this sample, Brad and Julie use some propaganda techniques when presenting their opinions. Both Brad and Julie think they are right about immigration. What do you conclude about immigration from this sample? Why?

As you continue to read through the viewpoints in this book, try keeping a tally like the one above to compare the authors' arguments.

CHAPTER 1

PREFACE: Should Illegal Immigration Be Stopped?

The borders of the United States are easily penetrated by illegal immigrants. Many thousands of people enter the United States illegally by simply walking across the border from Mexico or Canada. Others enter with permission and then stay in the United States past the time they are legally allowed.

While the United States government is aware of the problem, people disagree over how serious it is.

People who want to stop illegal immigration argue that the illegal immigrants hurt American citizens. They believe illegals take jobs away from citizens. They also argue that illegals use free clinics, put their children in public schools, and receive welfare. These people argue that such services are paid for by American citizens' taxes, and people who are not citizens should not be allowed to use them. The government should do more to control the borders, they argue, to try to stop illegals from entering.

On the other side are people who believe illegal immigrants help the United States. They say that illegals do not take jobs away from citizens because illegals take jobs most Americans do not want, such as dishwashing and other unskilled labor jobs. They also argue that illegals do not take advantage of free clinics and education because they are too scared of being sent home. Illegals do pay taxes and social security when they work, so they actually pay into the government but do not benefit from it.

Because illegal immigration is a very emotional issue, arguments for and against it use many propaganda techniques. In the next two viewpoints, look for examples of testimonial, card stacking, and scare tactics.

Illegal immigration should be allowed

Editor's Note: This article is paraphrased from an editorial written by Lou Cannon. Mr. Cannon is a reporter and an author in Washington, D.C. Mr. Cannon believes illegal immigrants help the United States. Note the propaganda techniques Mr. Cannon may use to support his argument.

The author lists only positive things about immigration. Which propaganda technique is this?

Does this testimonial offer a good reason to believe immigration is helpful to the U.S.? Why or why not?

Does this testimonial prove that illegal immigrants benefit society? Why or why not?

Illegal immigration is a large plus for this country, something we should be cheering, not criticizing.

Illegal Mexican immigration is a boon to our economy. And studies prove it. These immigrants pay heavy taxes (for which they receive no benefits). They make little use of welfare and other social services. Plus, they give far more to the United States than they take. As social scientist Wayne Cornelius said:

> It could be argued that Mexican migrants are a big help to the United States. They are young, highly productive workers, whose health care, education, and other costs have been paid for by Mexico.

These immigrants pay millions of dollars into Social Security that they will never collect. They also pay state income, sales, and even property taxes for which they receive few benefits. In the words of Douglas S. Massey of Princeton's Office of Population Research: "Far from ripping off the system, illegal aliens are more likely to be paying for it."

Mexican immigrants do not want to go on welfare. In San Diego County, it was found that out of 285,000 people who received Medi-Cal and food stamps, only 317 were illegal immigrants. Only 2.8 percent of illegals had collected welfare, and only 1.8 percent had received food stamps.

The Orange County Task Force found that illegal immigrants pay 83 million dollars in taxes each year. At the same time, they receive medical services costing only 2.7 million dollars a year. Mexican sociologist Jorge A. Bustamante believes these findings prove that illegal immigrants really should be called "illegal taxpayers."

One complaint against illegals is that they take jobs away from American workers. Another complaint is that they work at a lower hourly rate and are more easily taken advantage of. As U.S. Secretary of Labor Ray Marshall put it, they work "hard and scared." There are probably some instances where illegal immigrants fight for jobs with American workers. But studies prove that this fear is exaggerated.

In California, for example, both legal and illegal immigration is heavy. Yet, this state has the lowest unemployment rates.

More than half of the new immigrants head for the big cities, especially Los Angeles. The jobs they take, such as dishwashers or bus boys, are often the lowest paid.

Illegals may also work in skilled or semiskilled construction jobs, according to one study. They hold jobs as laborers, maids, janitors, and dishwashers.

Some economists believe that many of the jobs performed by illegals simply would not exist if the illegals were not in the market.

Illegal immigrants usually work in low-paying positions that American citizens refuse to do. Wayne Cornelius says that the illegal is willing to take the "unstable, dead-end position" because it helps his family. Also, many immigrants want to return to Mexico and so do not want to build careers in the U.S.

Bustamante believes that the growth of the Mexican population provides an ideal situation for the U.S.: In the U.S., there is a real need for cheap labor. In Mexico, there is an increasing population and dire poverty.

Migration from Mexico to the United States is here to stay, no matter what kind of fence is built on the border. And this immigration, in countless ways, is a real and lasting benefit to the United States.

What evidence does the author present to prove this issue is exaggerated? Is this enough proof?

Do you think *all* illegal immigrants would be willing to work at jobs like this? Is this argument a propaganda technique? Why or why not?

Has the author proven this statement?

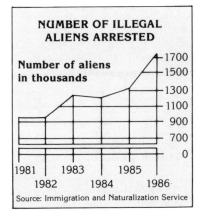

NUMBER OF ILLEGAL ALIENS ARRESTED

Number of aliens in thousands

1700
1500
1300
1100
900
700
0

1981 | 1982 | 1983 | 1984 | 1985 | 1986

Source: Immigration and Naturalization Service

Does illegal immigration help the U.S. economy?

Mr. Cannon believes illegal immigration benefits the U.S. in many ways. Name three of these ways. Which of these three do you think is the most convincing? Why?

Editor's Note: The following viewpoint is paraphrased from a brochure from the Federation for American Immigration Reform (FAIR). FAIR is a national organization that wants to end illegal immigration in the United States. While reading this viewpoint, keep in mind the three propaganda techniques the author may include.

The authors call immigration a danger and say Americans suffer because of it. Which propaganda technique are they using?

Are these people in a position to offer an informed opinion on immigration? What are their credentials?

Does the testimonial from this seamstress make a good argument against illegal immigration? Why or why not?

The authors give examples of illegals and citizens fighting and hurting each other. By giving the reader only one side of the story, what propaganda technique are the authors using?

Uncontrolled illegal immigration is a real danger to minorities and poor people of the United States.

These Americans pay the highest price for illegal immigration. Millions of illegal workers fight for jobs along with minorities, youth, and women.

The former National Urban League president Vernon Jordan said that illegal immigration "makes it tougher for citizens to find jobs or to demand decent working conditions." And Secretary of Labor Ray Marshall has said that there would be a lot more jobs if illegal immigrants did not take so many jobs Americans need.

Many employers would rather hire illegal immigrants because they can be taken advantage of. As just one example, FAIR'S office received a call from a seamstress. Her boss asked her to train a new employee, an illegal immigrant. Our caller was black, she was poor, and, as soon as she finished training the illegal worker, she was fired. She lost her job because her employer was able to pay the illegal immigrant less than she was paid.

Some people argue that illegal immigrants are only taking hard, dirty jobs that Americans do not want. The truth is that many Americans already work in these low-paying jobs. These Americans can be taken advantage of more easily when illegal immigrants also work in these jobs. This is because an employer can pay illegal workers less, offer illegals fewer benefits, and know they will not complain.

By taking away jobs that Americans need, illegals cause tensions to explode. In Chicago, Mexican-Americans and illegal Mexican immigrants began shooting each other while competing for work and housing. *The Washington Post* blamed Miami riots on the huge number of Cuban and Haitian refugees, because these refugees have taken jobs from native workers.

Uncontrolled immigration does not just threaten America's poor, however. *All* Americans suffer because of it.

Every year, half of the U.S. population growth is caused by immigration. While Americans try to have smaller families, immigration threatens our nation. If immigration rates continue to be this high, more than seventy million people will be added to the U.S. population in just fifty years, with no end in sight.

Every person added to our population drains our natural resources and contributes to the destruction of our environment.

In a Pulitzer-Prize-winning study, the *Des Moines Register* found that for every person added to our population, 1.5 acres of the richest farm land goes out of production to make way for new houses, roads, and shopping centers. If this continues, the U.S. will stop shipping food to other countries shortly after the year 2000. How can the U.S. feed the hungry people of the world?

Does *anyone* benefit from the rising tide of illegal immigration? Businesses that can profit from employing illegals at low wages do. And many illegals are better off here than in their own countries. But many others are exploited by dishonest employers and are treated like slaves. These immigrants are denied the rights and privileges we want every person in the United States to enjoy.

> **How could you check these statistics to make sure they are not examples of card stacking?**

> **The authors' conclusion is frightening. What propaganda technique is it?**

Pressure Points
Areas of Most Illegal Entries Into U.S.

SOURCE: U.S. News and World Report

Should illegal immigration be stopped?

The authors of this article use all three propaganda techniques in their argument to prove that illegal immigration harms American citizens. Even though the authors use these techniques, do they make a good case against illegal immigration? Can you name one argument in this article that you think proves that illegal immigration is harmful? Explain why you think it is so convincing.

Identifying Propaganda Techniques

After reading the two viewpoints on illegal immigration, make a chart similar to the one made for Brad and Julie on page 10. List one example of each propaganda technique from each viewpoint. A chart is started for you below:

FAIR:

SCARE TACTICS

Uncontrolled illegal immigration is a real danger to the minorities and the poor people of the United States.

Cannon:

CARD STACKING

Half a dozen studies prove illegal immigration benefits the U.S. Immigrants pay heavy taxes and pay little into welfare.

After completing your chart, answer the following questions:

Which article used the most propaganda techniques?
Which argument was the most convincing? Why?

CHAPTER 2

PREFACE: Should Legal Immigration Be Restricted?

Just about every American can quote from American poet Emma Lazarus's poem that appears on the base of the Statue of Liberty:

> Give me your tired, your poor,
> Your huddled masses yearning to breathe free,
> The wretched refuse of your teeming shore,
> Send these, the homeless, tempest-tossed to me,
> I lift my lamp beside the golden door!

At the time the Statue of Liberty was placed in New York harbor, America was looking for new immigrants to settle this vast, unoccupied land. America was a country that supposedly welcomed the dissatisfied, rejected, and oppressed people of other nations. Yet, even then, there were critics of immigration.

Today, there are still two sides to the immigration debate. Those who support continued open immigration believe it benefits the U.S. every bit as much as it did in the 1800s. They argue that immigrants create jobs and become productive, consuming citizens. These supporters believe the U.S. should open its arms to immigrants.

There are others that strongly disagree with this position. They believe that the U.S. can no longer afford to be as generous with its resources as it has been in the past. Immigrants contribute to high unemployment rates and overpopulation, and they use welfare and other free social services, critics argue.

The next two viewpoints reach opposite conclusions but use very similar arguments. Take note of the propaganda techniques each author uses.

Editor's Note: The following viewpoint is paraphrased from an article by Joseph P. Martino. Mr. Martino works for the Research Institute at the University of Dayton in Ohio. He has degrees in physics, electrical engineering, and mathematics. In this viewpoint, he tells why he believes immigration does not need to be controlled. As you read, try to detect any propaganda techniques Mr. Martino may use.

WHERE DO MEXICAN IMMIGRANTS WORK?

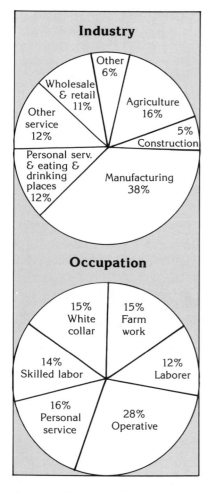

Source: Rand Corporation, 1986.

People who want to limit immigration argue that immigrants take U.S. natives' jobs. The arithmetic seems simple. For every immigrant who enters the country and takes a job, there is one less job for a worker who was already here. Opponents of open immigration believe that even if immigrants do not take American workers' jobs, they end up on welfare and become a burden to those who have jobs and pay taxes.

What about America's role as a refuge for those in need? Immigration's opponents think that the U.S. can no longer afford to play this role. They argue that the United States is no longer a frontier. Our resources are already scarce and our own problems are already so large that we cannot allow millions of new immigrants to come here.

For these reasons, the U.S. government is urged to limit or even end immigration. But are they good reasons?

The idea of legal immigrants taking other workers' jobs needs to be looked at closely. Abraham Lincoln once remarked that every person is created with two hands and one mouth, and he believed that the Creator intended those two hands to feed that one mouth. His idea is important to the issue of immigrants and unemployment.

Let's consider a typical primitive economy. In this economy everyone has a job—even the children and the old folks. For the healthy adults, it is a backbreaking job with long hours. Unemployment is unheard of. Yet the *economy* has not provided those jobs. All the people in that economy use their two hands to feed their own mouths, so each person creates his/her own job. The match is perfect: two hands producing and one mouth eating. Immigrants need work and their two hands can provide it. So the immigrant creates a new job while providing a worker to fill it.

This can be seen when immigrants enter the country and homestead farms, as millions did during the nineteenth century. Where did this farming job come from? Immigrants brought the jobs with them. They ate what they grew, and they grew it because they needed to eat. The economy did not make that job any more than a primitive economy makes the jobs in it.

Opponents argue that we no longer have a frontier to absorb millions of immigrants. This farm example may have worked a hundred years ago, they say, but it does not work any longer.

But this simple picture of immigrants settling on the frontier never was true. If we check out the history of immigrant groups in America, we find something very different.

In reality, most of the immigrants to the United States did not settle the frontier. Instead, they crowded into the cities, where they found and held jobs.

Immigrants are able to find room in our economy. Julian Simon in *The Ultimate Resource* argues that within three months of their arrival in the United States, 47 percent of Vietnamese males aged fourteen or older had obtained jobs. Simon also shows that when illegal Mexican aliens were removed by the Immigration and Naturalization Service from jobs they held in California, no native-born Americans could be found to fill those jobs.

This is a good example of immigrants creating their own jobs, not taking them from native workers. They were taking jobs that native workers, *including the unemployed,* did not want. As Tom Bethell, writing in *National Review* put it, "Illegal aliens are good at . . . slipping into all sorts of nooks and crannies, sometimes taking two or three part-time jobs."

So "jobs" are clearly not a good reason for limiting immigration. Instead, unemployment would probably end overnight if we simply got rid of the rules that prevent or discourage citizens from creating jobs.

This makes it sound as though more and more immigration might improve everyone's life. In fact, Simon has shown that people begin to benefit society about thirty years after they are born. In the case of immigrants, the payoff usually comes sooner. Legal immigrants, because many arrive as adults, begin becoming productive citizens right after they arrive. The payoff from illegal immigrants is even higher since they pay taxes but do not get Social Security and other benefits.

Is the author's comparison a good one? It sounds reasonable, but is it?

The author makes immigration in the cities seem easy and positive. Is this a propaganda technique? Why or why not?

Does Mr. Bethell's testimonial prove the author's point? Does Bethell sound like an authority?

The author states that immigration may improve everyone's lives. How?

Does this mean that we ought to throw open the gates and let anyone enter who wants to? We might very well be better off for doing that. The point here is simply that whatever we do about the level of immigration should not be done relying on the standard arguments about jobs and resources. They are false to the core.

MY GRANDFATHER CAME TO THIS COUNTRY IN 1897...

...HE AND GRANDMAMA WORKED DAY AND NIGHT TO SEND MY FATHER TO SCHOOL!

FATHER WENT INTO BUSINESS. WORKED HARD AND MADE HIS WAY UP.

I JOINED FATHER AND TOGETHER WE WON OUR SHARE OF THE AMERICAN DREAM!

BUT THESE CUBANS, HAITIANS AND MEXICANS FORGET THE DIFFERENCE BETWEEN GRANDFATHER AND THEM...

...THEY'RE TOO LATE!!

TAYLOR
ALBUQUERQUE TRIBUNE 80

© Taylor/Rothco

Does immigration harm America's natives?

State two reasons the author gives for believing that immigrants do not deplete jobs or natural resoures. Do you think these arguments are convincing? Can you name one fact from another article in this book that contradicts Mr. Martino?

Editor's Note: The following viewpoint is paraphrased from a speech Richard D. Lamm made in New York. Mr. Lamm is the former governor of Colorado. He argues that the U.S. must begin to severely control immigration.

The world has gone through a revolution and it has changed a lot.

We have cut the death rates around the world with modern medicine and new farming methods. For example, we sprayed to destroy mosquitoes in Sri Lanka in the 1950s. In one year, the average life of everyone in Sri Lanka was extended by eight years because the number of people dying from malaria suddenly declined.

This was a great human achievement. But we cut the death rate without cutting the birth rate. Now population is soaring. There were about one billion people living in the world when the Statue of Liberty was built. There are 4.5 billion today.

World population is growing at an enormous rate. The world is going to add a billion people in the next eleven years—224,000 every day. Experts say there will be at least 1.65 billion more people living in the world in the next twenty years.

We must understand what these numbers mean for the U.S. Let's look at the question of jobs. The International Labor Organization projects a twenty-year increase of 600 to 700 million people who will be seeking jobs.

Eighty-eight percent of the world's population growth takes place in the Third World. More than a billion people today are paid about 150 dollars a year, which is less than the average American earns in a week. And growing numbers of these poorly paid Third World citizens want to come to the United States.

In the 1970s, all other countries that accept immigrants started controlling the number of people they would allow into their countries. The United States did not. This means that the huge numbers of immigrants who are turned down elsewhere will turn to the United States.

The number of immigrants is staggering. The human suffering they represent is a nightmare.

Are these statistics making the author's point, or are they an example of card stacking? How can you tell?

What propaganda technique is the author using?

Latin America's population is now 390 million people. It will be 800 million in the year 2025. Mexico's population has tripled since the Second World War. One third of the population of Mexico is under ten years of age.

These people look to the United States. Human populations have always moved, like waves, to fresh lands. But for the first time in human history, there are no fresh lands, no new continents.

We will have to think and decide with great care what our policy should be toward immigration.

At this point in history, American immigration policies are in a mess.

Our borders are totally out of control. Our border patrol arrests three thousand illegal immigrants per day, 1.2 million per year. *Two illegal immigrants get in for every one caught. And those caught just try again.*

Adding the numbers of legal and illegal immigrants, 50 percent of all U.S. population growth comes from immigration. We are taking in more people than all of the rest of the world combined. We need to control our borders. As every house needs a door, so every country needs a border. And yet, our borders are full of holes. We have clearly lost control over our future.

Our children will pay the price of uncontrolled immigration.

The United States is no longer an empty continent. When the Statue of Liberty was built, there were 58 million people in the United States. In 1984 there were 240 million people.

We have seen more people without jobs. We are not doing a good job with our own poor. The U.S. cannot and should not be the home of last resort for all the world's poor, huddled masses.

Supporters of immigration use many arguments to support their side. Let's look at a few of these arguments:

Illegal immigrants take jobs no Americans want.

The fact is that the average illegal immigrant arrested in Denver, Colorado, made more than seven dollars an hour. Many were making over 100 dollars per day. We identified 43 illegal aliens making 100 dollars per day as roofers, and we have 438 people registered in our employment services who would love those jobs. The average illegal immigrant arrested in Chicago makes $5.65 an hour. More than thirty million American workers make less than that.

The author states we are losing control over our future. Does he prove this, or is he using scare tactics?

Another myth cited by supporters of immigration is that illegal immigrants work hard, pay taxes, and do not go on welfare. The sad truth is that these folks seem to learn the ropes of the welfare system with incredible speed.

Today's illegal immigrants apply for and receive benefits from the government that citizens need. Illinois did a study showing that it paid $66 million in unemployment benefits to illegal immigrants in one year, despite a law that was supposed to stop illegal immigrants from getting unemployment benefits. Los Angeles guesses that it spends 269 million dollars in social services on illegal immigrants each year.

This issue will not go away. Other generations of Americans made great sacrifices so that we today can enjoy the freedom, the quality of life, and the standard of living that we have. When I think of what uncontrolled immigration will do to the dreams of my parents and grandparents, what it will mean to the future of my children, I realize that we will find a way to control immigration. Because we must.

This evidence contradicts statistics you have read elsewhere. How might you prove who is right?

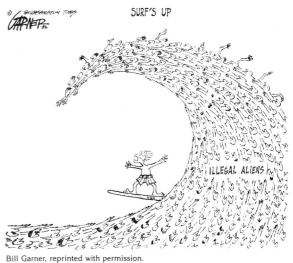

SURF'S UP

Bill Garner, reprinted with permission.

Should the U.S. control immigration?

List three reasons Mr. Lamm believes immigration harms the U.S. List three propaganda techniques Mr. Lamm uses in his viewpoint. After reading this article, whom do you most agree with, Mr. Lamm or Mr. Martino? Give two reasons why you agree with the person you chose. Give two reasons why you disagree with the person you did not choose. What do you conclude about immigration? Does it help or hurt the U.S.?

CRITICAL THINKING SKILL 2

Identifying Propaganda Techniques

This activity will allow you to practice identifying the propaganda techniques you have been learning in this book. The statements below focus on the subject matter of this chapter, whether or not legal immigration should be restricted. Read each statement and consider it carefully. *Mark an S for any statement you believe is an example of scare tactics, a C for any statement that is card stacking, and a T for any statement that is a testimonial.*

If you are doing this activity as a member of a class or group, compare your answers with other class or group members. You may find that others have different answers than you do. Listening to the reasons others give for their answers can help you in identifying propaganda techniques.

EXAMPLE: If the U.S. keeps allowing immigrants to come here, there will not be any food left for the citizens that already live here.

ANSWER: S, scare tactic. The author is using fear that there will not be enough food to prove his point that we must stop immigration.

Answer

1. Most Third World people already want to come to the U.S. If we do not stop immigration, all of them will come here and Americans will be put out of work. _____

2. Richard Lamm, former governor of Colorado, thinks immigration must be stopped. He has said that floods of immigrants are taking away citizens' jobs. _____

3. Fifty percent of all U.S. population growth comes from immigrants. We take more people than all the rest of the world combined. If we keep doing this, we know it will lead to more U.S. citizens being out of work. _____

4. Immigrants cannot wait to get here and steal jobs and money from Americans. _____

5. America has always welcomed immigrants. Almost all of our citizens have parents or grandparents from other countries. All of these people found work easily and are very happy. This proves we should not restrict immigration. _____

3

PREFACE: **Does Bilingual Education Benefit Non-English-Speaking Children?**

One of the issues related to immigration is bilingual education. Bilingual education programs attempt to teach English to immigrant children by using both the childrens' native language and English. Many children of recently arrived immigrants speak English very little or not at all. In the past, and to a certain extent today, these children have been "mainstreamed," or placed in the regular classroom along with children who already speak English. Many people argue that children placed in an English-only classroom will learn English much more quickly.

People who disagree with this view argue that it is confusing and humiliating for a non-English-speaking child to be put in a classroom with English-speaking children. They believe these children need special help. They need to be taught in the language they understand and to gain English skills slowly. Once they can speak English well, they can be mainstreamed.

The next two viewpoints debate the reasons for and against bilingual education.

Editor's Note: The following viewpoint is paraphrased from an article by Raul Yzaguirre, a civil rights administrator. Mr. Yzaguirre is the former head of the National Council of La Raza, a group that works to help Hispanics in the U.S. Mr. Yzaguirre explains why he believes Hispanic children benefit from bilingual education.

Bilingual education is one of the major issues of the 1980s, and it is much misunderstood.

Let us begin with the basic facts. The mainstreaming of non-English-speaking children into English-only classrooms has never worked, is not working now, and will never work. We need to do something different, and facts prove it:

Out of every one hundred children who enter school, forty Chicanos and Puerto Ricans will not complete high school.

One third of Chicanos and Puerto Ricans twenty-five years and older have not completed high school.

About one of four Chicanos and Puerto Ricans have less than five years of formal education.

Chicanos and Puerto Ricans have a 100 percent greater chance of being expelled from school than whites do.

The number of Chicanos who are held back at least one year is eight times greater than the number of whites held back.

The old excuses that were used to explain why the system is failing to work for Hispanics no longer hold water. Excuses like: "Hispanics do not do well in school because they are not as smart as whites." "They like to stay in their own *barrios* and speak their own language" (as in "Jews and Blacks like to live in their ghettos"). "If the waves of immigrants would stop coming, there would be no language problem." Any intelligent person has thrown out these ideas like worn-out shoes. Yet there are many people who continue to blame the victim rather than deal with the causes.

Over 70 percent of non-English-speaking children are Hispanic. Studies have always proved that Hispanics are the nation's most under-educated minority, and the numbers quoted above prove this fact. English-only instruction is as bad for Hispanics as slavery was for Blacks.

Opponents of bilingual education attack it because they do not seem to understand what *bilingual* means. Bilingual means *two* languages. In other words, in a bilingual program, children will be

The author has given us several reasons why mainstreaming has not worked and pronounced it a failure—is he using card stacking?

Is this comparison a good one, or is it an example of card stacking?

taught in both their native language *and* in English. People who support bilingual education believe that it is the best method of teaching English. It is only common sense that teaching must build upon what the child already knows. And for 3.5 million children in this country, what they already know is a language other than English.

If children are not allowed to learn by using their own language, they will be playing catch-up for the rest of their educational lives. In fact, what the public education system has been saying to non-English-speaking children is: "What you know is worthless; what you are is worthless; you do not fit our norm, and we have no responsibility to help you."

But these issues are never discussed in an honest way. Instead, opponents of bilingual education try to use tricky arguments. They say that "foreigners" refuse to become "American." The critics also argue that bilingual education will lead to separate political and social beliefs for Hispanics.

Hispanics are not "foreigners." The language and culture of Hispanics are as deeply rooted in U.S. history as are puritanism and the English language.

Supporters of bilingual education have a clear goal: for non-English-speaking children to be able to use both their home language and English. The message is one of connecting, bridging, unifying the two cultures through language, not separation or isolation.

Have we become as a nation so afraid that we cannot accept a few of our children learning differently than others? Is our unity as a people so delicate that we must try to make every child into what we think every American should be and then label that child a failure when he or she does not measure up to that standard? There are rich rewards to having Americans who know more than one language and culture. Let's start realizing it.

The author cites what he believes happens to children when they are not taught in their native language. Do these consequences seem real, or is this an example of card stacking?

The author is using very positive words to describe bilingual education. Which propaganda technique is this?

Does bilingual education help children?

Mr. Yzaguirre is convinced that bilingual education is needed to keep Hispanic children from falling behind. State two reasons he gives for believing this is true. Mr. Yzaguirre's argument becomes very emotional at times, and he uses a few propaganda techniques. Give one example of a propaganda technique used by Mr. Yzaguirre to make his point.

Editor's Note: The following viewpoint is paraphrased from an article by Abigail M. Thernstrom, an author and specialist on educational issues. Ms. Thernstrom argues that bilingual education harms children more than it helps them.

Bilingual education looks right, but the program is all wrong. It harms Hispanic children instead of helping them. And it does so in programs that separate the children from their black and white peers.

There is no doubt that the school dropout rate for Hispanic children is high. About 70 percent never finish high school; only about 7 percent finish college. So it is clear that we should help Hispanic children, but I do not think bilingual education is the answer.

People who support bilingual education argue that classes taught in a child's native language help that child learn other subjects while learning English. But there is no hard evidence to support this view. In fact, the results from one important study seem to conclude the opposite.

The author lists only the harmful effects of bilingual education. Is this a propaganda technique? If so, which one?

First, the study found that most children in the bilingual program already knew English quite well before entering the program. This would suggest that these children could have been mainstreamed into the regular classroom without bilingual education. Second, of those who did not know English, bilingual education was not helping: These children had still not learned English. Third, the bilingual programs were aimed at keeping Hispanic children separated from their English-speaking peers. This would harm the children by isolating them and preventing them from learning English in other situations, such as on the playground. And finally, whatever language was being taught, children who started out "not fitting in" in school tended to stay that way. This proves that bilingual education does not help children to assimilate any better than if the program did not exist. As added proof against bilingual education, the study found no evidence that children in the programs were more willing to stay in school.

In spite of this study, bilingual education is still supported by many people. Why? The reason is clear: The programs provide employment and political opportunities. Schools are forced to hire Hispanics without regular teaching credentials. Also, Hispanic leaders and their supporters want to keep Hispanic culture separate from American culture.

This kind of separation ends up harming Hispanic and other non-English-speaking children. It prevents them from learning the English skills they need in order to compete and get ahead in education and employment. These children are at a disadvantage because they cannot relate to people outside their own culture.

These programs seem to deliver not more equal but more *un*equal education. By and large, bilingual education harms Hispanic and other non-English-speaking children. Bilingual education is failing to teach these children English. It is also failing to help them learn to get along with their English-speaking peers. These children then grow up to live in the same poverty that too many of their parents grew up with. It closes the door, in other words, to educational and economic opportunity.

Has the author supported her conclusion about the harmfulness of bilingual education, or is this a scare tactic?

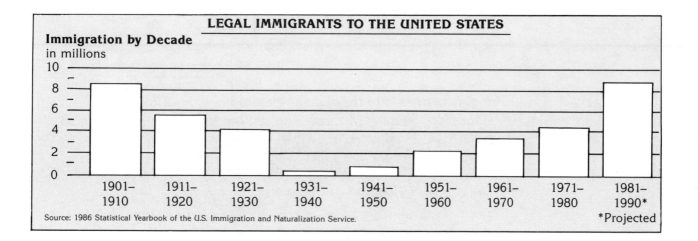

LEGAL IMMIGRANTS TO THE UNITED STATES

Immigration by Decade in millions

Source: 1986 Statistical Yearbook of the U.S. Immigration and Naturalization Service.

*Projected

Is bilingual education harmful?

Ms. Thernstrom uses many of the same reasons to prove bilingual education is harmful that Mr. Yzaguirre uses to prove it helpful. Can you name two? Which propaganda techniques did Ms. Thernstrom use? Give an example of each.

Understanding Editorial Cartoons

Throughout this book, you have seen cartoons that illustrate the ideas in the viewpoints. Editorial cartoons are an effective and usually humorous way of presenting an opinion on an issue. Cartoonists, like writers, can use ways of persuading you that include deceptive techniques. While many cartoons are easy to understand, others may require more thought.

The cartoon below is similar to cartoons that appear in your daily newspaper. It emphasizes a point made in the article that you read by Raul Yzaguirre: that words from other languages have become part of American culture. Look at the cartoon. How does it illustrate that point?

What does the cartoonist think of making English the official language? Can you think of words that you use every day that are based on other languages? Do you think it is true that English is a mixture of other languages? Why or why not?